my first

abc

from the Quran

Sadia Khan

Goodword

d dates

elephant

g

grapes

h hoopoe

jar

lamp

m mosque

n

Prophet
Nuh's ark

rain

tent

U

Uzayr's donkey

W well

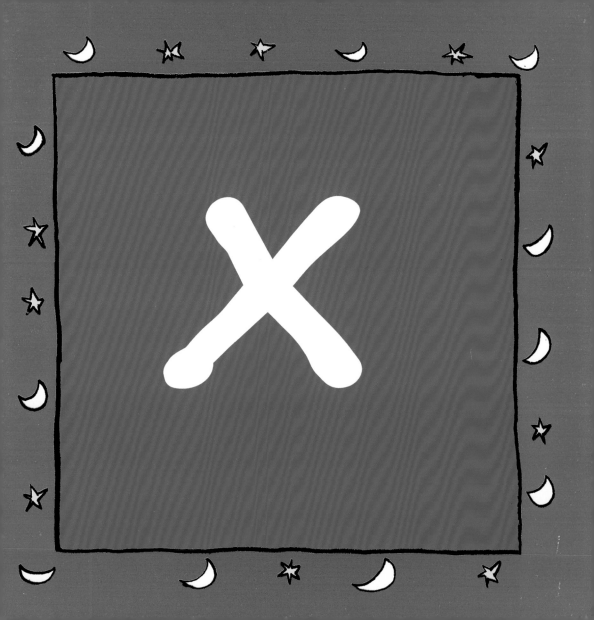

y

yellow
cow

a	ant (naml)	Surah an-Naml 27:18
b	bird (tayr)	Surah al-Baqarah 2:260
c	camel (ibil)	Surah al-Ghaashiyah 88:17
d	dates (qinwaan)	Surah al-Anaam 6:99
e	elephant (feel)	Surah al-Feel 105:1
f	fish (hoot)	Surah al-Araaf 7:163
g	grapes (inab)	Surah an-Nahl 16:11
h	hoopoe (hudhud)	Surah an-Naml 27:20
i	ink (midaad)	Surah al-Kahf 18:109
j	jug (ibreeq)	Surah al-Waaqiah 56:18
k	Kabah (house of God)	Surah al-Maaidah 5:95
l	lamp (misbaah)	Surah Fussilat 41:12
m	mosque (masjid)	Surah al-Araaf 7:31